"RETAKERS ESSENTIALS and SURVIVAL GUIDE"

This past exam had the lowest rate of bar passers in a decade, this according to all statistics. The reason for the drop in the pass rate is a point of argument, and depending on what side you are on, you may take one reason over the other.

In my research for this publication, what I have learned is that if this past exam is a precursor to future exams, then what used to work in preparation of passing the bar, is insufficient.

"July 1014 bar pass rate falls to near record low" (California Bar Journal)

"Texas sees decline in bar pass rate" (JD Journal)

In my talks with some law Professor's about what the examinee should do differently in preparation for the February 2015 exam and further, they all had a common theme, that is practice, and practice more.

Others indicated that they may point their students in broader areas of the law, because

A. THOMAS ARCHIIR

"RETAKERS ESSENTIALS and SURVIVAL GUIDE"

they and the examiners recognize historic legal events in the world, and the ever growing area of International Litigation, and its' impact on American Law, and its' judicial system.

No one can learn all 100,000 plus laws, but even if you could, that is not what the examinees are looking for. One professor who writes for the bar stated "I wrote the essay, and I know the answer I am looking for." Wow, powerful words being stated their but we must learn what they know, in order to please our graders and score high enough to pass the bar exam.

Right now in America an example can be found in the recall of over 5.4mm airbags manufactured and imported by outside vendors from other countries, the vendors appeared at one point to be denying the necessity of a recall to the extent requested, and comply with the wishes of our highest levels of government. Could this be a showdown where International Law could become a factor?

A. THOMAS ARCHIIR

"RETAKERS ESSENTIALS and SURVIVAL GUIDE"

Real world litigation that in the past has not been an area of concern for examinees, and maybe will not be now. However when you truly understand what it is you are attempting to accomplish, that is becoming an American Lawyer, then this complex legal matter may be something you should at least peruse, and just maybe you will learn something of value. Some may call this legal fiction learning, and to that I say, learn as much legal fiction as you can.

Legal Fiction

In fact I am of the belief that when in doubt look for the law, logic, and facts, for an appropriate response, but also you must understand the power of "legal fiction," and when, how, where, or if, you should apply this powerful knowledge on your exam.

The term "legal fiction," is generally defined as: An assumption that something has occurred or someone or something exists which, in fact, is not the case, but that is made in the law to enable a court to equitably resolve the matter before it. In order to do justice, the law will permit or create legal fiction. *Legal Dictionary by Farlex 2014*

One recent use of legal fiction appears in a recent law suit filed against the state bar of California.

On the cover of the pleading, listed under the words Defendant's appears the word ROES 1-50. My first thought was this was a typo, but then I remembered the attorney is a prominent attorney with national recognition, and the defendant is the State Bar of California.

Most of us are readily familiar with the term DOES as it applies to legal pleadings, but ROES...

For some of you this may be a poor example of legal fiction, but on the exam when posed with essays that include, Urbania, or other fictional statements as facts, researching words such as ROE, could have provided for you a vein of other similar legal fiction words.

A. THOMAS ARCHIIR

Unfortunately, and unmistakably, this is the reality in which we are being tested today, and learning this area of law, may be the only thing you can use in a pinch, that at least has a resemblance of legal authority.

Alternative Legal Perspectives

This concept is exactly what I am writing to you about, in the hopes of getting you prepared to address far-fetched alternatives of the law, that you may not have studied in the past. I hope they will provide the examinee essential alternative legal perspectives which I feel you must, or at least should know.

What that means to the examinee is that one bar preparation company will not be enough to hoist the examinee to the score required to pass, and that they must find and add alternative educational sources and applications to what once was as simple as ABC.

For this reason, the examinee should know of all sources of what you may consider alternative bar preparation companies. This means that the test taker MUST be familiar with all styles of test taking formats.

If you are a repeater, one style is not enough, so think about adding other sources of bar preparation like, Themis, BarMax, Adaptibar, Kaplan, CaliforniaBarHelp.com, Fleming, 1440calbarhelp, etc.

There are many sources available to you, so check them out, try to find a fit, and learn from them, even if it is just one thing to ad to your toolbox.

One of my professors uses the toolbox analogy quite often when teaching his students. He talks about the toolbox of an electrician, a carpenter, and a auto mechanic.

One common tool in all of the toolboxes is the screwdriver, and a wrench probably cannot be used in making a cabinet, just like a sander cannot be used for changing a tire.

So prepare your own tool box, but remember what you will be working on, might require all of the tools to make it work for the exam.

By adding more than one bar tutor while studying will place you in the best possible situation on exam day to pass, because you will be familiar with more than one method, and thought process. The bar exams can differ greatly, and learning how to approach each individual essay question, will provide you with more options on how to write for that question.

Preparing for the MBE

For those who were not competitive at the MBE this means that more than one source of study material must be applied. I have done nearly 10,000 practice questions and answers myself, but before this fact scares you, I must say that many of them were repetitive, and came from one comfortable source, meaning comfortable to me to read and understand.

But you must learn out-side of your Comfort Zone when practicing this essential part of the exam.

A. THOMAS ARCHIIR

"RETAKERS ESSENTIALS and SURVIVAL GUIDE"

There are many different authors of practice questions, with different grades of difficulty.

On this past exam, the questions were brutal and appeared to be from only one source, that is the most difficult practice questions available. It would have done no one any good to have studied just the easy ones, or just those in your comfort zone.

One thing I found that helped me to learn intricate parts of the rules of law was to read the answers provided at the end of the MBE preparation book, as part of my study regimen.

From reading all of the answers, that provided me with a better understanding of the laws and rules that I already understood, and defined them better for me.

By doing this, I also found little known exceptions that better prepared me to address with confidence those little known facts of law if they appeared on my exam.

A. THOMAS ARCHIIR

"RETAKERS ESSENTIALS and SURVIVAL GUIDE"

Another important thing you will learn from the MBE questions is your particular area of weakness in learning the law. Many of the computerized ones show a graph that breaks down all of the subject areas of law, and the sub areas of law.

I can remember that one that bugged me the most was formation under contract law. One of my professors told me a story that his ABA school barley covered contract law, and for this reason, all he could do was tell me where to find the law.

So each subsection must become familiar to you, and while no one can memorize the 100,000 plus laws, you are not expected to, but your weak areas of law must be brought up to a competitive level in order to give you the very best chance at success on your next exam.

Learning from conflicts in application of the law

When listening to audio in preparation for the exam, you may find conflicts in interpretations of key points of law, or different reasoning behind the legal concept.

Whether you decide to agree with one side or the other is up to you, however remembering and understanding what the other professor is saying is a must, because what they are saying may be the only correct answer available on the exam.

As for me, my professors are from all over the country, many who have passed the bar in more than one jurisdiction. What I have learned independently is that what may work for an examinee in New York, or Maryland, may not work in Nevada, or Oregon.

My understanding is that essays for the exams, are written by our of state professors, and while we all have the common law, and the UCC, what the examiners will allow, can be tantamount to the verbal accents from the different regions of English speaking countries.

This goes to the reality that, what you write, is just as important as how you write it.

A. THOMAS ARCHIIR

"RETAKERS ESSENTIALS and SURVIVAL GUIDE"

I would hope by now, that you recognize that it is essential to make the grader of the exams work as easy as possible. By writing using shorter paragraphs, then both underlining and highlighting shows professionalism, from you and respect for the grader.

To prepare and have the best opportunity to pass this next bar exam, the examinee must be open to learning more theories and applications of law.
Because on the exam, one theory or application may not fit perfectly, but another will.

By doing this you will find differences in legal argument, and on the exam, if what you learned does not fit, another angle of the same area of law may.

Before you can trust other sources, you must confirm new areas of law that you learn, the jingle is "learn it and confirm it," this confidence building process can go a long way, especially under the stress of the bar

A. THOMAS ARCHIIR

examination.

You can also learn and build confidence by utilizing Google, and the plain text rule when looking to find the law, this does work, and for students who are not already familiar with "Secondary Sources," familiarize yourself with this essential area and source of learning. CALI lessons offers an interactive tutorial specifically on this major growth area of learning, and preparing for the bar exam.

This all goes to the heart of diversity, and preparation. Learning one major point of law from secondary sources, can tie up a lot of lose-ends in your understanding of the law, but be careful to not go overboard on it.

Making difficult interpretations

One of my additional or alternative law professors likes to use these foreign or weird names for the actors names in his essays. This used to drive me crazy, making me think "can't you just keep everything simple," after all you are naming the parties.

"RETAKERS ESSENTIALS and SURVIVAL GUIDE"

While reading with comprehension necessary to understand the essay, I now had to worry about how to pronounce this name, or think of another name to give that actor, all while watching my clock.

What I have subsequently learned is that this is a very effective way to teach what you will probably face on the bar exam, and studying before hand will allow you to understand and thus react to the style of the author, and what is expected from you in order to pass.

As I mentioned before the professor knows the model answer, this is true for the bar graders too, so you just as well practice writing essays with the funny city, or weird actors names in them, and be better prepared for those weirdo's, when you see them on the bar exam.

If you are a "retaker then you know the testable material that will be given on each day of the exam, meaning that Monday's exam consists of these applications, Tuesday of this and Wednesday of that.

A. THOMAS ARCHIIR

"RETAKERS ESSENTIALS and SURVIVAL GUIDE"

While practicing, place yourself mentally in the exam at that time, keep an eye on your clock, then realize what area of law you are missing, or what is lacking now in your knowledge. It is better to find that out now, remember it, correct it, and apply it.

The authors of the exam, have months, and years to write these exam questions, and you only have an hour to answer them, so be prepared to overcome this temptation, or lazy way out.

Understanding the difference between the words, shall, must, could, may, as they apply to legal writing, and understanding of the law is essential. So make sure you do know these differences when you read them and when to use them, one word can make a difference, especially if you have to use it over and over again. Knowing this difference between correct usage when writing, and incorrect usage can make a difference.

A. THOMAS ARCHIIR

The legal memorandum

Memorandum writing is alive and well at the bar examination.

I hope by this time in your preparation, that you are familiar with how to write all areas and styles that will be tested, and that you practice writing all of the different styles, thus on exam day, you will be familiar with all of the different styles and formats in which you will be tested.

The "Memorandum," (performance tests) requires attorney style skills to complete, and is the most over-looked practice by law students, according to my many sources.

For this reason, you may want to look at getting a tutor, who has a specialty in this type of writing You must not ignore it, if you do, you may find yourself learning it for the next exam, and note this portion of the exam may vary by jurisdiction.

"RETAKERS ESSENTIALS and SURVIVAL GUIDE"

Whether your bar exam is two or three days long, you should know your itinerary for each day, and then study using this sequence.

Learn by practicing in the way you will be tested. If it is writing first, then multiple choice, then study that way, because familiarity-breeds-comfort, I personally believe that statement to be true.

About the writing software

The July 1014 aftermath of the exam included alleged problems with the software used to capture the examinees work-product.

Obviously, during the exam many things are beyond the control of the examinee, and those things should not be of concern during the exam.

For those brave enough to hand-write the examination, it was not a concern then, or perhaps at all now.

Personally, I tip my hat to those who choose

"RETAKERS ESSENTIALS and SURVIVAL GUIDE"

to hand-write in this day of technology...

If you are using a computer on the bar exam, it is essential that you familiarize yourself with the software before the date of the exam.

This is very important because the features of underline, bold, and italicize should be used in your presentation to the grader of your work.

By learning how to work the software, you can easily go back to a previous exam, maybe to cut-and-paste, or to make sure you remembered to write a key point of the previous exams.

Learn how it works now, familiarize yourself with all available functions, such as spell check, and auto-correct.

While in the middle of my exam, I recalled that earlier when writing on a Murder, on a previous essay, I suddenly remembered that I had failed to define Homicide. This omission could have failed my entire exam, but I knew how to get back to that essay, because I had practiced, and beat up the software while in the comfort of my own home. Thus I was able to go back to that earlier saved essay with confidence, and I added my definitions of Homicide, then moved, back to the middle of my other essay.

Do not be afraid to call the manufacturer of the software and ask questions. I did, and the wait was not too long, and the representative seemed knowledgeable, patient, and willing to assist.

Allow yourself a chance to learn

Additionally, you MUST make time to STUDY, and the easiest way to do this is to study in a method or approach that will allow you to learn.

Some people are readers only, and do not, or, cannot listen to the lectures or definitions via audio publications, but instead must read them to understand, or are more comfortable just reading, or vice-versa. Just like reading is important, audio is just as important, because

"RETAKERS ESSENTIALS and SURVIVAL GUIDE"

the same way you learn to sing the words to your favorite song, can be applied to learning and recalling the law.

For others who audio provides their best learning environment, you must read, and learn how exam passers are formatting the passing essays, see every period, comma, and high-lighted areas. Remember, Success, breads success, and you must help yourself, at every opportunity, and learn what you must learn to pass, no exceptions!!!

With respect to the difficulties in our understanding of the law and issues, which occurs sometimes, one of my favorite professors states; "you have no choice but to understand it."

So make sure when preparing that you find a way to understand what you are reading, because on the exam, you will be faced with far-fetched facts, with many actors, and laws, but by practicing the difficult readings now, you will have the mind set and confidence to remain competitive during the exam.

A. THOMAS ARCHIIR

"RETAKERS ESSENTIALS and SURVIVAL GUIDE"

With any level of higher education, what you learn and how well you learn it for that particular field could become easier, if you understand the format in which the learning is instructed, and thus learned.

If you are reading this for the first time, and have never taken the bar exam before, preparation and details of the smallest type, are essential, just ask anyone who has been in your passed the exam before, or is retaking it.

I wrote this publication in the hopes of providing a thought process for you to succeed. My other publications on this very subject, I share specifics that I have learned, that you must too, to give yourself the best opportunity to succeed, at the end of the day, that is really anyone can ask for.

I wanted to take this opportunity to thank you, and all of my Colleagues from Harvard. And a special thanks to all of my law professors from around the country, Jay, George, Steve, Mary, Aaron, Jeff, David, and

A. THOMAS ARCHIIR

"RETAKERS ESSENTIALS and SURVIVAL GUIDE"

Alan, thanks for your help!!!

LEADERSHIP EXCELLENCE IMPACT

This author is an alumni of:
Harvard Kennedy School

In this publication the author has shared and, covered what was learned from a multitude of sources, and the reason why what used to be common protocol for exam takers, is may

A. THOMAS ARCHIIR

have changed for the foreseeable future.

Just as in the early to mid-seventies when many bars added more areas of law to be tested perhaps here the changes are in the required application, by means of complex communications that must be conveyed to the grader, in order to avoid having to prepare for the exam once again.

This publication is for educational purposes only, and represents my experience. The examinee or reader must remember this is their own examination in which they are preparing for.

I would strongly suggest that as such, you must prepare using many sources of information that are available, due to the ever-changing examination thresholds being presented, and thus required and expected contents for passing exam answers.

Because of this I recommend using the many alternate methods of learning academic law as a good solid foundation, and remember

"RETAKERS ESSENTIALS and SURVIVAL GUIDE"

this, learn-it-then-confirm-it, the law that is...

Please realize that the results of your exam, is in your hands, and preparation, repetitiveness, and legal logic MUST become a substantial factor if you are planning on passing your Bar Examination.

GOOD LUCK TO YOU IN YOUR 2015 BAR EXAMINATION!!!

A. THOMAS ARCHIIR

www.ingramcontent.com/pod-product-compliance
Lightning Source LLC
Chambersburg PA
CBHW070737180526
45167CB00004B/1790